S0-ATK-103

Library

THUNDERSTORMS

BILL McAULIFFE

CREATIVE EDUCATION · CREATIVE PAPERBACKS

THUNDE

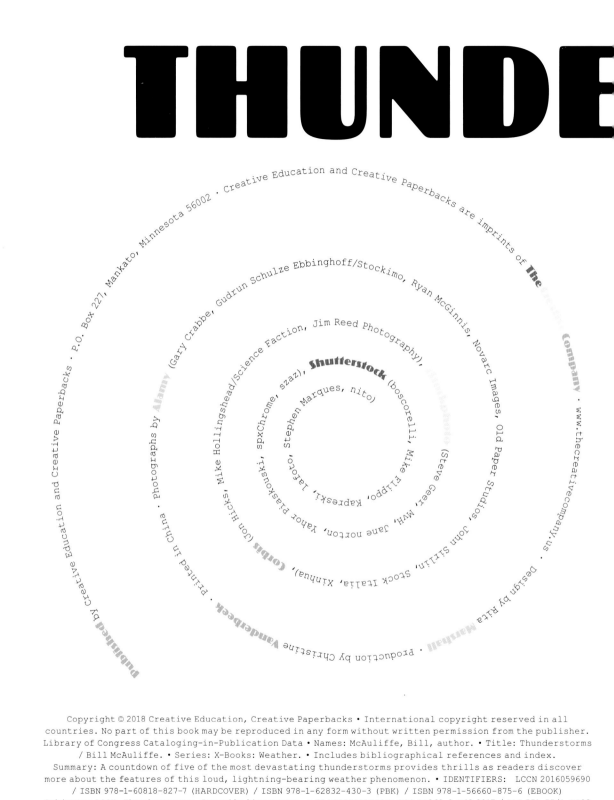

Published by Creative Education and Creative Paperbacks • P.O. Box 227, Mankato, Minnesota 56002 • Creative Education and Creative Paperbacks are imprints of The Creative Company • www.thecreativecompany.us • Design by Rita Marshall • Production by Christine Vanderbeek • Printed in China • Photographs by Alamy (Gary Crabbe, Gudrun Schulze Ebbinghoff/Stockimo, Ryan McGinnis, Novarc Images, Old Paper Studios, John Sirlin, Stock Italia, Xinhua), Corbis (Jon Hicks), Dreamstime (Steve Geer, MVH, Jane norton, Yahor Piaskouski, sxpxChrome, szaz), Newscom (Mike Hollingshead/Science Faction, Jim Reed Photography), Shutterstock (boscorelli, Mike Filippo, Kapreski, lafoto, Stephen Marques, nito)

Copyright © 2018 Creative Education, Creative Paperbacks • International copyright reserved in all countries. No part of this book may be reproduced in any form without written permission from the publisher.

Library of Congress Cataloging-in-Publication Data • Names: McAuliffe, Bill, author. • Title: Thunderstorms / Bill McAuliffe. • Series: X-Books: Weather. • Includes bibliographical references and index. Summary: A countdown of five of the most devastating thunderstorms provides thrills as readers discover more about the features of this loud, lightning-bearing weather phenomenon. • IDENTIFIERS: LCCN 2016059690 / ISBN 978-1-60818-827-7 (HARDCOVER) / ISBN 978-1-62832-430-3 (PBK) / ISBN 978-1-56660-875-6 (EBOOK) Subjects: LCSH: Thunderstorms—Juvenile literature. • CLASSIFICATION: LCC QC968.2.M43 2017 / DDC 551.55/4—DC23 CCSS: RI.3.1-8; RI.4.1-5, 7; RI.5.1-3, 8; RI.6.1-2, 4, 7; RH.6-8.3-8
First Edition HC 9 8 7 6 5 4 3 2 1 • First Edition PBK 9 8 7 6 5 4 3 2 1

RSTORMS

Xtraordinary
WEATHER 5

Xciting
FACTS 28

Xtreme
TOP 5 THUNDERSTORMS

#5 10
#4 16
#3 22
#2 26
#1 31

Xtensive
DAMAGE 24

Xceptional
THUNDERSTORMS

Xasperating
STORMS 10

GLOSSARY

RESOURCES

INDEX

WEATHER X BOOKS

THUNDERSTORM CHARACTERISTICS

RAIN THUNDER LIGHTNING

Thunderstorms have complicated recipes. Warm air, moisture, and wind are key ingredients. They combine to make thunderstorms. Some are destructive. Nearly all are spectacular.

Thunderstorm Basics

The National Weather Service (NWS) puts out warnings when thunderstorms approach. There are good reasons for that. Thunderstorms bring rain, thunder, and lightning. Some feature strong, straight-line winds or hail. These forces can damage property or injure people.

The most basic type of thunderstorm is a single-cell storm. This short-lived event lasts about half an hour. Multi-cell thunderstorms are the most common. These storms can last for hours. Squall lines are long, narrow bands of storms. They pass quickly.

AMERICAN LIGHTNING DEATHS, 1959—2015

Of those struck by lightning, 90 percent survive. Many do not remember being struck. They often suffer burns and bruises and are knocked unconscious or paralyzed.

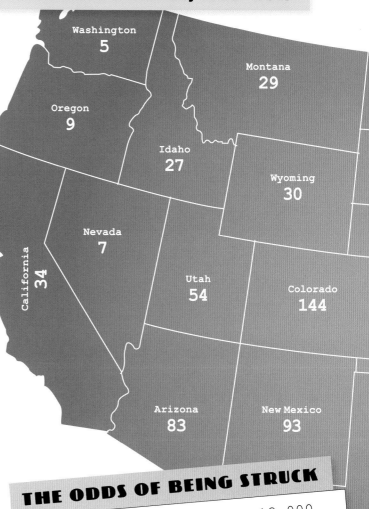

Washington
5

Montana
29

Oregon
9

Idaho
27

Wyoming
30

Nevada
7

California
34

Utah
54

Colorado
144

Arizona
83

New Mexico
93

Alaska
0

THE ODDS OF BEING STRUCK

by lightning are about 1 in 13,000.

ONLY ABOUT 10 PERCENT

of lightning occurrences hit the ground.

ON AVERAGE, 9 OR 10 PEOPLE

are killed by lightning in Canada each year.

Hawaii
0

LIGHTNING STRIKES THE UNITED STATES

about 25 million times per year.

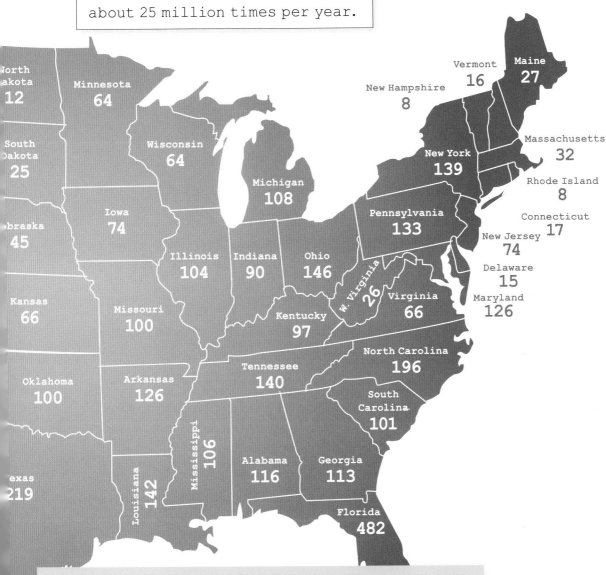

North Dakota 12
Minnesota 64
Vermont 16
Maine 27
New Hampshire 8
Massachusetts 32
South Dakota 25
Wisconsin 64
New York 139
Rhode Island 8
Michigan 108
Connecticut 17
Nebraska 45
Iowa 74
Pennsylvania 133
New Jersey 74
Illinois 104
Indiana 90
Ohio 146
Delaware 15
W. Virginia 26
Virginia 66
Maryland 126
Kansas 66
Missouri 100
Kentucky 97
North Carolina 196
Oklahoma 100
Arkansas 126
Tennessee 140
South Carolina 101
Mississippi 106
Alabama 116
Georgia 113
Texas 219
Louisiana 142
Florida 482

CANADIAN LIGHTNING DEATHS, 1921–99*

British Columbia: 16 • Alberta: 107 • Saskatchewan: 133

Manitoba: 78 • Ontario: 316 • Quebec: 206 • New Brunswick: 39

Prince Edward Island: 2 • Nova Scotia: 24 • Newfoundland and

Labrador: 2 • Nunavut, Northwest, and Yukon territories: 0

*excludes 1959–64

UPDRAFTS & DOWNDRAFTS

Each thunderstorm cell has one updraft and one downdraft. These powerful winds move quickly up and down within a storm. They can be faster than 80 miles (129 km) per hour.

The most feared type of thunderstorm is a supercell. Supercells are huge, rotating storms. They can last for hours and move independently of the wind. Supercells can be hundreds of miles wide. They often produce hail more than two inches (5.1 cm) wide. Their updrafts can be more than 150 miles (241 km) per hour. About 20 percent of supercells produce tornadoes.

supercells are the number-one producer of tornadoes.

SUPERCELL STORMS

Of the approximately 2,000 thunderstorms happening on Earth at any moment, 2 are supercells.

Xtreme Thunderstorm #5

Johnstown Flood In the spring of 1889, heavy rains fell over Pennsylvania's Conemaugh Valley. On May 31, Lake Conemaugh pushed through the South Fork Dam. A wall of water and debris more than 30 feet (9.1 m) high raced through the valley. It hit the city of Johnstown at 40 miles (64.4 km) per hour. The flood killed 2,209 people. It remains one of the greatest losses of life in U.S. history.

The U.S. experiences around 100,000 thunderstorms per year.

About 10 percent of those storms are severe.

Thunderstorm Formation

A thunderstorm starts with the sun. Sunlight heats the earth, pulling water vapor upward. The moist, rising air cools. Then it **condenses** into tiny water droplets. The droplets gather to form a puffy, white **cumulus** cloud.

The cloud can build six to eight miles (9.7–12.9 km) high. Up there, the air is so cold that the water droplets freeze. This makes hail. When the hail gets heavy enough, it falls through the cloud's updraft. It often melts into heavy rain on the way down. Meanwhile, strong winds might blow the top of the cloud off in one direction. This forms the classic **anvil** shape of a mighty summer thundercloud.

Within the cloud, bits of water and ice collide, creating **static electricity**. A **current** of electricity can form within a cloud or between the cloud and the ground. This is lightning. It forms in an instant. Lightning quickly heats the air around it. The heat causes a shock wave of rapidly expanding air. That creates a sound wave known as thunder.

SINGLE-CELL THUNDERSTORM about 30 minutes; heavy rains

MULTI-CELL THUNDERSTORM 30–60 minutes per cell; high winds, hail, flooding, weak tornadoes

SQUALL LINE 10–20 miles (16.1–32.2 km) wide; high winds, heavy rains, hail, tornadoes

SUPERCELL more than 60 minutes; high winds, large hail, flooding, strong tornadoes

THUNDERSTORM FORMATION FACT

Lightning and thunder occur at the same time. But light moves much faster than sound, so people see lightning before they hear thunder.

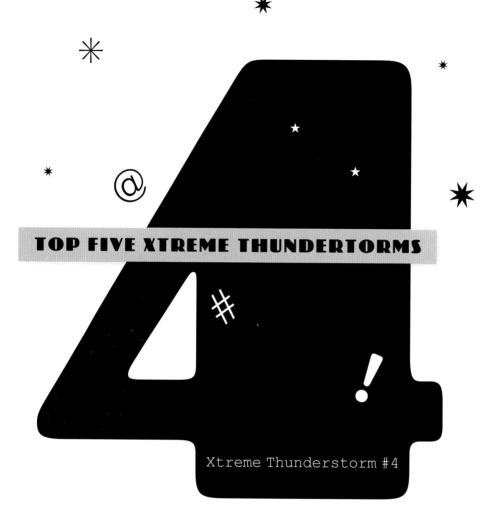

Xtreme Thunderstorm #4

The Tristate Hailstorm swept from Kansas to Illinois on April 10, 2001. As it traveled across Missouri, it hit Kansas City, Columbia, and St. Louis. Hail ranged from one to three inches (2.5–7.6 cm) in diameter. It was driven by 70-mile-per-hour (113 km) winds. Nearly every home in Florissant, Missouri, was damaged. In all, the storm caused $1.5 billion in damages. At the time, it was the costliest hailstorm in U.S. history.

APRIL 10, 2001

XCEPTIONAL THUNDERSTORMS

In the Northern Hemisphere, most thunderstorms occur in June, July, and August. In the Southern Hemisphere, thunderstorms are more frequent in December, January, and February.

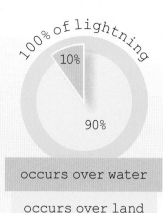

100% of lightning

10%

90%

occurs over water

occurs over land

THUNDERSTORM OCCURRENCES FACT

Lake Maracaibo in Venezuela gets thunderstorms about 297 days each yea

It has more lightning than any other place on Earth.

Thunderstorms can form at any time of the year.

THUNDERSTORM FORMATION

Thunderstorm Occurrences

Florida is nicknamed the "Sunshine State." But it has more thunderstorm days than any other state. This is because it is surrounded by water. Winds from the Gulf of Mexico and the Atlantic Ocean collide over Florida, forming storm clouds. The five U.S. cities with the most thunderstorm days each year are all in Florida.

Some of the worst thunderstorms in the U.S. occur in the Midwest. Dry air from the Rocky Mountains meets moist air from the Gulf of Mexico over the Great Plains. They crash into each other. This often creates massive squall lines or dangerous supercells. These storm systems can be hundreds of miles long. They can produce straight-line winds in excess of 100 miles (161 km) per hour. Or they can quickly spin into violent tornadoes.

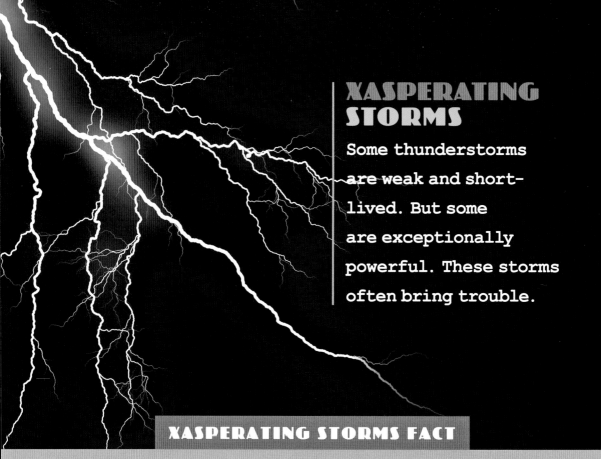

XASPERATING STORMS

Some thunderstorms are weak and short-lived. But some are exceptionally powerful. These storms often bring trouble.

XASPERATING STORMS FACT

In the spring and summer, most severe thunderstorms occur from southern Minnesota to Texas. They can be difficult to predict.

A severe thunderstorm watch is put out when conditions are right for one to develop. A severe thunderstorm warning is put out when one is already occurring.

Thunderstorms can produce heavy rain. That rain can flood cities and fields alike. Floods kill more people each year than tornadoes, hurricanes, and lightning combined. Thunderstorms can also drop hail. Hail can range from the size of a pea to the size of a softball. It can break windows, dent cars, damage roofs, and ruin crops.

Powerful wind gusts can sweep along the ground during a storm. Wind can knock down trees and power lines. A nearby clap of thunder can cause hearing damage. Lightning can reach 55,000 °F (30,538 °C)—five times hotter than the surface of the sun. It can start a fire wherever it strikes.

The most dreaded product of a thunderstorm is a tornado. Tornadoes are typically small. But their winds can spin more than 200 miles (322 km) per hour. They can travel long distances. Violent twisters can flatten anything in their path.

TOP FIVE XTREME THUNDERSTORMS

Xtreme Thunderstorm #3

Mid-Atlantic Derecho Straight-line winds from thunderstorms can cause tremendous damage. These walls of winds are sometimes called derechos. They quickly march hundreds of miles. Derechos level trees and buildings. In June 2012, a derecho traveled from the Midwest to the Atlantic coast. Its peak winds were 91 miles (146 km) per hour. It killed 13 people and left 4 million without power for a week. The storm caused $3 billion in damages.

JUNE 29, 2012

XTENSIVE DAMAGE

The Storm Prediction Center (SPC) in Norman, Oklahoma, issues thunderstorm watches for the U.S. Using current weather conditions, it forecasts the risk of severe storms developing.

Severe Thunderstorms

Any thunderstorm can cause damage. Even those that are not severe can bring lightning, thunder, small hail, and heavy rain. A storm is considered severe if it has hail one inch (2.5 cm) or larger. If it has wind gusts of at least 58 miles (93.3 km) per hour, or if it brings a tornado, it is also labeled severe.

The SPC categorizes the risk of severe weather. The lowest is described as marginal. This means winds could reach 60 miles (96.6 km) per hour. Hail up to one inch (2.5 cm) wide could fall. The chance of a tornado developing remains fairly low until the risk becomes moderate to high. Then, the risk of any tornado forming increases from 30 to 45 percent. As the chance for severe storms increases, so does the risk of danger and damages.

SEVERE WEATHER RISK

Category 1	Marginal (isolated severe thunderstorms possible)
Category 2	Slight (scattered severe thunderstorms possible)
Category 3	Enhanced (numerous severe thunderstorms possible)
Category 4	Moderate (widespread severe thunderstorms likely)
Category 5	High (widespread severe thunderstorms expected)

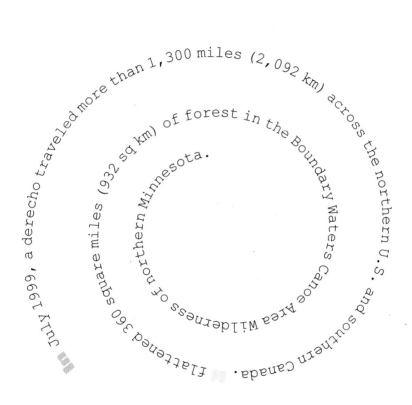

July 1999, a derecho traveled more than 1,300 miles (2,092 km) across the northern U.S. and southern Canada. Flattened 360 square miles (932 sq km) of forest in the Boundary Waters Canoe Area Wilderness of northern Minnesota.

SEVERE THUNDERSTORMS FACT

Derechos travel at least 250 miles (402 km).

Their winds regularly gust more than 74 miles (119 km) per hour.

Xtreme Thunderstorm #2

Saguenay Flood The Canadian city of
Saguenay had two weeks of steady rain in
July 1996. Then nearly a foot (0.3 m) of rain
fell in two days. That led to flash flooding
and mudslides. Houses were swept away by
the rushing water. Ten people died. Another
12,000 were forced out of their homes. Some
neighborhoods were submerged under eight
feet (2.4 m) of water. It was Canada's first
$1-billion natural disaster.

JULY 19–21, 1996

Benjamin Franklin proved that lightning was made of electricity in 1752.

Lightning strikes Canada about 4 million times each year.

Thunderstorms are a basic element of most forms of severe weather.

Fear of thunder is known as brontophobia. Fear of lightning is keraunophobia.

When a storm brings thunder and snow at the same time, it is called thundersnow. Thundersnows are rare.

The central U.S. and eastern Australia experience more supercells than other parts of the world.

Lightning strikes Earth about 45 times per second.

Every flash of lightning carries enough energy to operate a 100-watt light bulb for 3 months.

About 80 percent of people killed by lightning are men.

More than 500 people study weather at the NWS's National Weather Center in Norman, Oklahoma.

Hurricanes generally do not produce lightning and thunder because they do not have vertical winds.

A wall cloud of dust in a desert thunderstorm that reduces visibility to nearly zero is known as a haboob.

Lightning bolts are usually one or two inches (2.5–5.1 cm) wide.

Dry lightning occu:

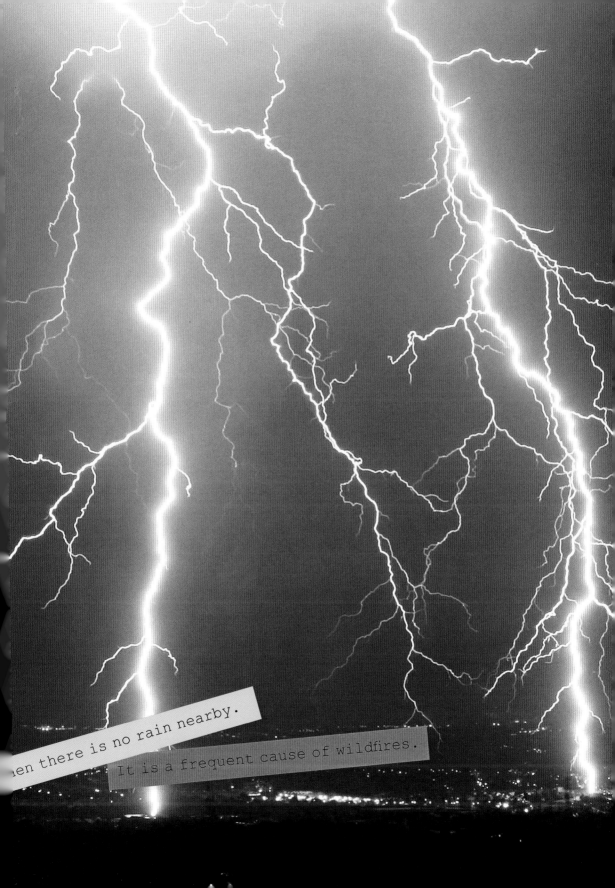

...en there is no rain nearby.

It is a frequent cause of wildfires.

MAY 5, 1995

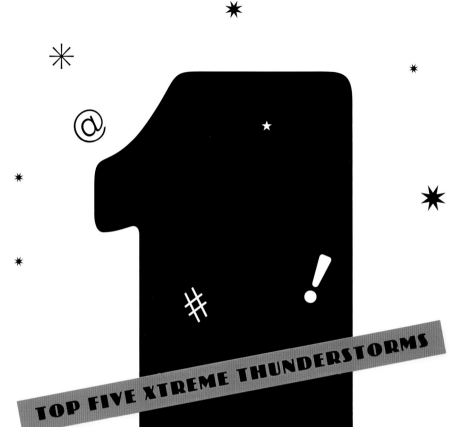

Xtreme Thunderstorm #1

Mayfest Storm The first $1-billion thunderstorm in U.S. history hit Fort Worth, Texas, in May 1995. It brought almost everything a thunderstorm can. It had softball-sized hail, heavy rains, flash floods, and straight-line winds of 70 miles (113 km) per hour. Flooding killed 16 people. Another person died from a lightning strike. At an outdoor festival, hundreds of people were injured by hail. Roofs collapsed. Crops were ruined.

GLOSSARY

anvil – a heavy steel or iron block with a flat top, concave sides, and typically a pointed end, on which metal can be hammered and shaped

condenses – changes from a vapor into a liquid

cumulus – a low-level, moisture-laden cloud; typically forms during summer and often produces storms

current – in electricity, a flow of electrical charges

static electricity – the buildup of an electrical charge on an

RESOURCES

Douglas, Paul. *Restless Skies: The Ultimate Weather Book*. New York: Sterling, 2005.

Kahl, Jonathan. *First Field Guide: Weather*. New York: National Audubon Society, 1998.

Lynch, John. *The Weather*. Buffalo, N.Y.: Firefly Books, 2002.

National Severe Storms Laboratory. "Severe Weather 101— Thunderstorms." http://www.nssl.noaa.gov/education/svrwx101 /thunderstorms/.

Palmer, Chad. "A Look Inside a Thunderstorm." *USA Today*. http://usatoday30.usatoday.com/weather/tg/wtsmwhat/wtsmwhat.htm.

INDEX

categories 5, 8, 12, 20, 24, 25

death tolls 6, 7, 10, 22, 26, 31

derechos 22, 25

formation conditions 5, 12, 18, 19

haboobs 28

infamous thunderstorms 10, 16, 22, 26, 31

lightning 5, 6, 7, 12, 15, 18, 21, 24, 28, 31

National Weather Service 5, 28

Storm Prediction Center 24

supercells 8, 9, 12, 19, 28

thundersnows 28

thunderstorm features 5, 8, 20, 21, 22 , 24, 31

tornadoes 8, 12, 19, 21, 24

A "clap" of thunder is a sudden sound lasting 0.2 to 2 seconds.